I0449434

THE INDIAN'S PONY

Bikágí Yishtłizhii Bilį́į́'

Susan Fadler

Library of Congress Card Tx-364-811

February 26, 2001

1st Printing October 15, 1995

Second Printing June 20, 2015

ISBN # 978-1-329-23495-6

Copyright June 20, 2015

Author: Susan Fadler

Publisher: Lulu Printing

Visit: www.ruffprogram.com

THE INDIAN'S PONY

Bikágí Yishtłizhii Bilį́į́'

With special appreciation to:

Chinle Curriculum Center

Gloria Means

Rudy Begay

Patrick Begay

Dean C. Jackson Center for Navajo Culture and Studies

Marjorie Thomas

Darlene Redhair

Peter Thomas

Resource Specialists

Will Tsosie

Mike Mitchell

Culture Teachers

Lorraine Begay

Pat Denny

Best Friends Animal Sanctuary

The Wilson Foundation

Educational Consultant

Dr. Ted. P. Fadler

Veterinarian

Dr. Janet Forrer

THE INDIAN'S PONY

Bikágí Yishtłizhii Bilį́į́'

1st Place Winner of the 1996 Prestigious ASBA Golden Bell Award

Wild Stallion!

After we moved to Chinle in 1990 into our apartment we found out where to shop for food, where to fill our water jugs, and where to take our garbage.

I know that sounds odd to many of you, but it was a necessary step as there was no garbage collection available, and wouldn't be for another year. No one wants garbage sitting around; it draws flies, mice, rats, and in Chinle, dogs.

Once every few days we would all pile into our four-wheel drive Jeep and head to the landfill. Fires were usually burning inside of it and when it was full, town workers covered it up and dug another one. The landfill is gone now and a modern garbage service is in force, but during this period this is how it was.

One evening after dinner we set out for the landfill. It was just about dusk when we pulled off the paved road and turned onto the powdery dirt road that went past a very old burial ground, down a hill round a curve and up another hill before we arrived at the big hole. Large Juniper bushes lined the ridge on each side of the road where we stopped at.

We got out of our vehicle and everyone was carrying a bag of garbage as we headed over to throw them down the deep hole. We were talking about what had happened that day, chatting and laughing. My daughter, Amanda, and my husband Ted, threw their bags in then turned to head back to the car. Just as my son, Jason, and I were ready to leave, there was a loud cracking of branches as a large reddish-brown stallion charged out of the Juniper bushes into the clearing at us. He was a spectacularly beautiful horse with a large white blaze down his face and four white stocking feet. The rays of the evening sun were shining on him giving Jason and I a good view before we turned and ran.

He was not a friendly horse.

The mustang came at us around the side of the pit. Ted and Amanda were back at the Jeep. Ted started the engine and opened the doors seeing what was happening. Reaching the Jeep Jason and I got inside and slammed the doors, not a moment too soon either because the horse was right on us.

The stallion reared up at the vehicle and pawed at the air with his hoofs and let out a wild scream that sent shivers up your spine. It was the first time I had ever seen a wild stallion and a sight I'll never forget. There was no mistaking his intent – he wanted us out of there in no uncertain terms.

My husband tried to move our Jeep forward a little and then tried to turn it around so we could leave but that stallion wouldn't give an inch. He charged the Jeep again and this time he nearly brought his hoofs down on the hood of our vehicle. If we got stranded there we'd be in very big trouble. Ted threw the car into reverse and started backing down that winding curvy road as fast as he could go with the stallion chasing us. All of us were very quiet not knowing what was going to happen.

The horse's ears were laid flat back against his head which was turned slightly to one side. The whites of his eyes were showing as he continued screaming, snorting, and pawing at the ground. Finally at the last curve he quit chasing us. He shook his head turned around and galloped back.

He'd won. He chased off our vehicle and the humans in it.

Later, I talked to some other people who'd had the same experience with that stallion. It seems he staked out that territory around the landfill as his and all comers were met with the same challenge. I was told he brought his band of mares and foals down from the mountains and plateaus every fall and had a reputation as being very aggressive. It was not a good idea for anyone to go to there alone.

I don't know what ever happened to that fabulous stallion, he was a sight out of the old west, a true treasure, so wild, so free. I will always remember him. How he protected his herd of mares and foals, doing what nature intended for him to do challenging even vehicles. I'm grateful no one was hurt. The stallion's intent that evening was to drive us off. He certainly accomplished his goal.

Dedicated to all the environmentalist and biologists who are trying their best to keep the wild mustang free and in the wild for all to see and enjoy.

To my family – what an adventure we had ~

A RUFF MISSION

1. GOAL: An intention to bring about a more clear understanding of the Indian Pony or "Wild Horse" also called "Mustang" which was so much a part of our countries rich culturally diverse culture and to achieve a civil and social lesson.

Problem Statement: Unfortunately, there are not many wild Mustangs left. Many have already been rounded up by helicopter which frightens the horses making them run so hard some collapse from exhaustion, some fall and break legs, instances where young colts were run so hard their hoofs fell off. A government agency, Bureau of Land Management or BLM said there is nothing wrong with this type of behavior. The people they hire to do this type of rounding up turn a blind eye to suffering of these animals. According to the National Academy of Sciences 2013 report they say there is no evidence of horse overpopulation and these roundups are unjustified. The BLM says there is evidence of overpopulation. If the horses need to be rounded up should they be subjected to abuse?

2. Measurable behavioral objectives: Students will show they understand the idea presented visually, orally and written text where applicable. This RUFF Mission is civic minded and encourages students to become involved. The fate of these wild mustangs is a good example of how they can voice their opinions. Students will get "involved" by writing to their congressmen, tribal leaders, the BLM, even to the President of our country and express their opinion on how to HELP the wild mustangs.

http://www.blm.gov/wo/st/en/prog/whbprogram.html

3. Specific strategies to help a student focus on character building: Trust. Respect; Responsibility; Fairness; Caring; Citizenship. These are ethical values to guide our choices. The standards of conduct that arise out of those values constitute the ground rules of ethics, and therefore of ethical decision-making. The ethical values act as a multi-level filter through which to process decisions. Being trustworthy is not enough — we must also be caring. Adhering to the letter of the law is not enough — we must accept responsibility for our actions or our inactions. Good character can help us detect situations where we focus so hard on upholding one moral principle that we sacrifice another — where, intent on holding others accountable, we ignore the duty to be compassionate; when intent on getting a job accomplished, we ignore how it's done. Good character can dramatically improve ethical quality of our decisions, our character and our lives.

Character questions about the way wild horses are treated:

- Are the wild horses being dealt with properly? If so, why? Or, why not?

- What is the wild horse and burro act? What was it based on?

- Do you agree with the way the BLM rounds up the horses? Is it necessary?

- Do they know what a Medicine Hat horse is?

- Why was a Medicine Hat horse so desired, why were they considered special?

4. An awareness or level: Getting students to respond, get involved and understand the plight of this American icon is the best thing we can do for the future of the Mustang.

For example in 2011, a 12 year old student made a documentary video titled: Free to Roam? The Mustang Debate" that describes the debate over the wild horse and burro management. While this debate has resulted in many articles and videos, what's unusual about this video is that the producer was a 12-year-old student.

https://www.youtube.com/watch?v=MLoBQmNtm9U&feature=youtu.be

Brigit Brown of Moriarty, New Mexico, turned a project for National History Day in her school into an award-winning documentary. The film won first place in regional and state competitions, and was featured at the Supreme Extreme Mustang Makeover in Dallas, Texas, in September 2011. But – did this film go far enough? Does a stronger statement for the Mustangs need to be made– by a student or students encouraging government officials to listen? Does she support the BLM or not in her video?

Learn what probability is – use the question below:

Write Fun Math Probability Activity on board

Ask: How likely is something to Happen?

Problem in percentage:

They see a herd of Mustangs in the wild. There are 3 pinto horses, 5 white horses, 3 black horses, 4 buckskin horses and 2 white horses. When you move a little closer to the herd of horses they disappear behind large rocks. What is the probability of seeing two pinto horses first? Answer: Out of a total of 17 horses, 3 are pinto horses. The probability of seeing a pinto horse is 3/17, .176, or 17.6 percent.

Write names of professions that use probability. Example: Many scientists and social scientists use probability, including epidemiologists, psychologists, economists, and statisticians. They predict outcomes of events, such as the incidence of diseases and the strength of the stock market.

Problem: Do they think the BLM agency is using probability to determine the fate of the Mustangs?

Ask students to look up the current arguments that the BLM makes over the horses on their website. Have the students read what the animal rights groups say about the horses or the use of data, such as statistics and probability. Then have them analyze the use of the information. Why did the BLM use this data? What points were effectively made about the pros and cons of the horses? Was the data useful on the horses? Did the data strengthen the argument? Have students provide evidence to support their ideas.

Our kids are the future.

- They can begin NOW. Encourage them to write to their government agencies.
- Have them get answers from agencies like the BLM.
- Have them let the BLM know if they this it is right to drive horses by helicopter.
- What do they think about the horses being injured on these drives? Is there a better way?
- If a sixth grader can make a video like the one mentioned above what can they do to help the Mustang?
- Watch the video with your students then ask then to share their opinions. Ask them to write down what they feel is wrong, if anything, with it. Have them tell you what they think is being done the correct way.
- Ask students if they think horses are native species to the United States? Make sure they understand native species.
- Ask them if native species should be protected?

6. Student practices: Writing letters and expressing opinions by getting involved should be crucial for all Americans. This country was built on **"we the people."**

- Have students talk to their parents. Share with them how they feel about mustangs being driven off the land. Ask them to watch the video with their parents.
- Ask students if they think the Mustang is a symbol for the United States? Do they think the Mustang interferes with grazing for cattle and sheep?
- Should areas of land be reserved for the Mustang?

- The Mustang was the Indian's Pony. It was important in culture, in stories and in history. Is this a part of America's history, our history?
  - Is it possible that in the future the mustang could be gone in the wild?
  - What would we lose if that is allowed to happen?
  - Publish their articles, stories in school and parent newsletters.
  - Make a video

7. Suggested questions are included at the end of the text. (Outcome based) These questions are meant to stimulate lively discussions in your classroom. Students should be encouraged to state opinions. What should be done with the last remaining Mustangs that still roam in the wild? Some groups maintain that taking too many Mustangs off the range reduces their genetic pool, thereby putting them at another risk. Do the students understand what is meant by genetic risk? Put the students in groups of 4 or 5 and give them a question to work on then start the discussion.

8. Navajo words are included in the text and on a separate list to enrich students and make them aware of another culture. This language was being spoken before any white man ever came to this continent bringing his language with him. It is not the idea to be able to speak these words, it is the thought of another's way of life, a different culture and that English is not always someone's primary language.

9. This text is appropriate for 6th grade and up, other ages for use by teacher discretion. There is a huge amount of material here. Use it for writing projects, civil government projects, classroom speaking etc., video projects, character building, doing the right thing even though it sometimes goes against what others want.

The Indian's Pony

Navajo language and Indian culture added for enrichment

Horses, łį́į́', have always held a special place in the lives of Native Americans. Even today, the horse is valued in everyday life. Horses meant wealth, jit'į́, to many tribes. Horses were used to barter for items and were given as gifts.

Below is a little of the written history, at least what is taught to us about the coming of these horses to the Native American Indian tribes . . . is it accurate? Or were the horses here before? Some say the horse is a native species, others disagree. What do you think?

Written history tells us that during the 1600's, Spanish people built many rancheros around the Santa Fe and Taos New Mexico area. On these rancheros they had thousands of horses. Native Indians were captured and forced into slavery by these Spanish land owners and made to work their rancheros. The Spanish government, fearing the Indian and a possible uprising, set a decree that forbid any native to own a horse. Some Indians however, learned of the Spanish horses by working around them. They learned how to handle horses and learned how to ride them. It is said that at first Indians were afraid of the sight of a horse with a man on its back, was this true? What we do know is that the Apache and Navajo tribes did steal horses from the Spanish rancheros.

Prior to the 1680 Pueblo Revolt, the only Indians familiar with or that possessed horses were the Apache and Navajo, Diné', who stole the Spanish horses. After the 1680 Revolt, numerous horses were said to be running loose on the plains once the Spanish abandoned the rancheros. By 1730 these horses had spread northward as far as Canada.

The <u>Comanche tribe</u>, Bitsii' yishbizhii, had established themselves by 1706 after they started to raid the Spanish rancheros and steal their horses. Their raids became legendary. The Comanche has a saying: "we let Spaniards stay in Texas just to raise horses for us." Their warriors continued going into Mexico to steal more horses, even after the Spaniards left, just to insult the Spanish.

It is believed the Comanche stole about thirty thousand horses a year from Mexican rancheros. The month of September became the month when large raiding parties went to Mexico after horses and captives. Comanche referred to September as the Mexican Moon; Mexicans called it the Comanche Moon. Other tribes especially the Apaches began to copy the Comanche and conducted their own horse stealing raids into Sonora and Chihuahua.

History tells us that the Comanche Indian was the essence of what the <u>Plains Indians</u>, Bikágí yishtł' izhii dine'í, Horse Culture became famous for. Texans had a saying that went something like this: "A white man rides a Mustang until the horse is played out – a Mexican will rides a Mustang another day until he thinks he is tired – but a Comanche will ride his Mustang to where he is going."

By 1760 the military leaders from Mexico believed the Comanche warrior on horseback to be the supreme fighter. Comanche warriors emerged as the primo horse traders between other tribes and French settlements east of the Mississippi. Horses had now spread from the southwest in two directions: north to the <u>Shoshone,</u> Abitsii Yishbizhii, then to the <u>Nez Perce</u>, Bíchįįh bighá hoodzánii, <u>Flatheads</u>, and the <u>Crow,</u> Gáagii dine'é, then to the <u>Kiowa</u>, Halgai hatííl dine'é, <u>Pawnee</u>, Halgai hóteel dine'é, and to the cousins of the Pawnee, the <u>Arikara</u>, or Sahnish dine'é.

Early Map of Indian Ponies Distribution

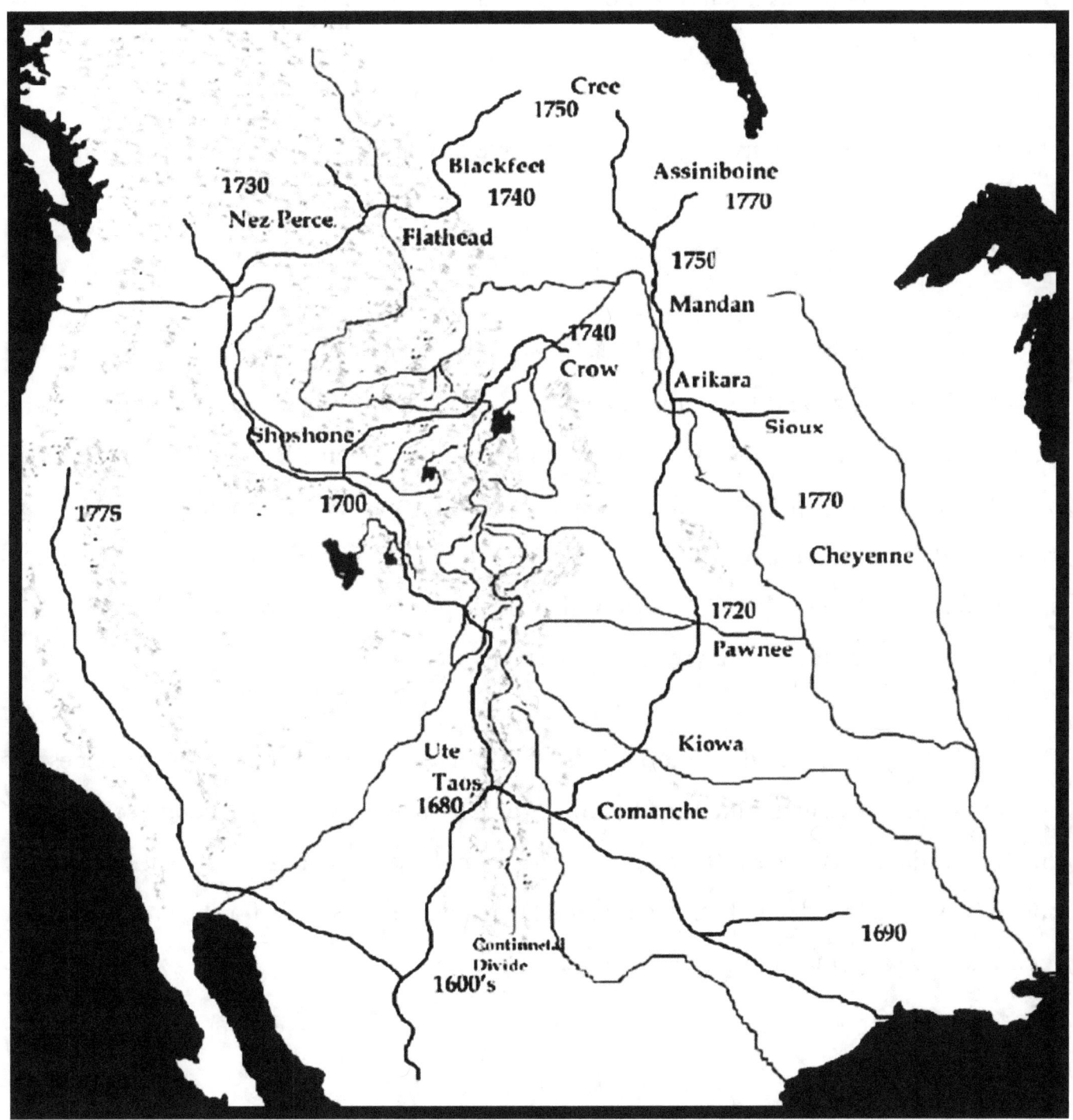

In this RUFF Curriculum, The Indian's Pony, we are talking specifically about the Mustang, the wild horse and an icon of the American West, the horse that has contributed to so many of the breeds that are known today. It is also a horse that is still running wild. Government agencies are rounding them up. This horse has an amazing ability to survive, to thrive in the wild.

Some people view it as invasive, as a feral horse and think it should be exterminated.

Others believe it should be saved and be allowed to run wild and free.

Government agencies use probability to determine the size and number of horses. Effective wild horse and burro management is dependent on accurate population counts and defensible assumptions. The Bureau of Land Management (BLM) routinely uses the probability assumption that wild horse and burro herds increase annually at an average rate of 20%. However, an analysis of BLM data for 5,859 wild horses found that approximately 50% of the foals survived to the age of 1 year, which indicates a 10% population growth rate based on yearling survival rates.

Data and analysis is based on the BLM's wild horse and burro removal and processing documents acquired under the Freedom of Information Act by environmental scientists in 2014. The data sets were evaluated separately, and then combined to total 5,859 wild horses, captured, aged, and branded by BLM. This data is the basis for the analysis in this report and the accompanying chart table.

Table 1 Age Structure Yearling Survival Rate

Herd Area	ROUNDUP DATE	HORSES PROCESSED PER FOIA	TOTAL FOALS CAPTURED	% OF FOALS	TOTAL YEARLINGS CAPTURED	% OF YEARLINGS	SURVIVAL RATE OF FOALS REACHING ONE YEAR
Calico	Dec 2009-Jan 2010	1848	378	0.2045	248	0.1342	0.6561
Twin Peaks	Aug-Sept 2010	1535	302	0.1967	147	0.0958	0.4868
Triple B	Jul-Aug 2011	1226	243	0.1982	134	0.1093	0.5514
High Rock/Fox Hog	Oct-Nov 2011	1250	245	0.1960	81	0.0648	0.3306
Totals		5859	1168	0.7955	610	0.4041	2.0249
Averages				0.1989		0.1010	0.5062
				average herd increase using foal rate		average herd increase using yearling rate	average yearling survival rate

The BLM bases their management decisions on environmental assessments that cite inflated population estimates. As shown in this study and previous research, the BLM's assumption of a 20% annual wild horse population growth rate is not based in science; leading to unsubstantiated population estimates with no evidence of excess wild horses.

Questions:

- What do you see in the chart above? Is this argument valid?

- Looking at the chart above - if the average herd increase of 10% is due to the births of foals that live for at least a year and if the average wild horse lives to age 20. There is a 5% decrease in herd size due to natural deaths. What would the actual herd growth be for year?

Answer according to biologists "there is a tendency for mankind to want to place a fixed value on nature, whether it be population growth, or decline. Because nature is dynamic, and not static, fixed, and continuously adjusting values will always change. One year horse population growth may be 5%, and another year a decline, but it will always be in balance with predators and competitive grazers, based upon their numbers and the carrying capacity of the land. In other words we can't dictate what nature is going to do, or assume it will operate according to our plans. Population growth or decline will always fluctuate according to natures mechanisms. There will always be declines and always some growth, but it will bounce back and forth based upon the capacity of the land. Wildlife species populations will never, grow continuously, including the wild horse and burro populations. We have to get that concept out of our brains. There has been much said about wild horse populations trying to make these massive comebacks, after roundups. Yes nature does have a tendency," IF" the factors are there to make a comeback, but never continuous, or out of control. Sadly, after the roundups, so many of the wild horses are removed, bands are broken up, mares are sterilized and male female ratios are adjusted, by the BLM, that nature can never make a comeback. The only true answer is, stop the roundups, restore back to the wild all of the wild horses and burros, that are in holding, to the areas that they were taken from, they will settle back into their old lives and leave our hands off. Remove the restrictions on nature and let nature determine what happens." Robert C. Bauer, Biologist.

http://www.habitatforhorses.org/a-biologists-response-to-the-blms-wild-horse-problem/

If any pure mustang horses exist they might be rare today, but they use to run over the plains in great numbers. During the 1880's the US Calvary tried numerous times to wipe out the Indian's pony in documented evidence with complete massacres of these horses. This alone is silent witness to the toughness of this little horse. They are survivors, better than anything the cavalry could put up against them.

Mustangs in Indian Culture

Now, let's get to know more about this amazing horse, the Mustang and more importantly to discover why one particular mustang, because of its markings during the 1880's, became synonymous with the meanings of power, mystic, and magic.

It is said in Navajo cultural stories that all horses were a gift from the <u>Sun</u>, Jóhónaa'éí. The Sun then gave them to his sons; <u>Monster Slayer</u>, Naayéé Neizghání, and <u>Child Born of Water</u>, Tó Bájíshchíní, to bring them to the people. These special horses with many coat colors were important in Navajo life and culture, as they were in many other native Indian cultures. They were considered to be sacred beings.

Horse coat colors are still synonymous with the four sacred directions that are always said in this order.

- <u>East</u>, Ha'a'aah

- <u>South</u>, Sha'di'ááh

- <u>West</u>, E'e'aah

- <u>North</u>, Nahookos

The colors of the horses were also given special names and meanings:

- A <u>white horse</u>, łíí łgaii, was said to represent <u>White Shell,</u> Yoołgaii, and synonymous with the East.

- The gray horse, łį́į́ Łibéii, was said to represent Blue Bead, or Turquoise, Dootł'izhii, and it is synonymous with the South.

- Buckskin horses, abání, represented Abalone Shell, Dook'o'osłííd, also called the ear shell. The Buckskin Horse is synonymous with the color of yellow, łitso, the West.

- Black horses, łį́į́' łzhiin, represents Jet, Bááhzhinii, or Obsidian, Bááshzhinii, a black shiny substance formed by rapidly cooling lava. A Black Horse is synonymous with the North.

- The pinto, łį́į́łkiizh, was the most special colored horse. A pinto and had a certain mystique, it was the horse of many colors.

Horses of specific colors stood for wealth, knowledge, baa ákohonidzinii, and material goods, naalyéhé .

I held an interview with Will Tsosie, a Navajo historian, of Chinle, Ch'ínlį́, Arizona, which is located in the heart of the Navajo Indian Reservation near the mouths of Canyon de Chelly and Canyon del Muerto. I asked Will why this horse was so revered and why this it was considered to be magical to the Indian.

Will explained it to me this way.

"When an Indian was in possession of a horse in the coloration of a Pinto, he then had a <u>composite</u>, yee hadít'éii, of all the different characteristics and meanings of the others horse in <u>his horse</u>, biłį́į́', because it had all the other colors found in other horses. Every revered color was represented; ever sacred direction was honored. But the most revered horse within this desired pinto coloration was yet a very different, very special horse. It was a particular color type of a Mustang, the coloration of it's coat so valued that it was known by all different tribes of Native Indians, especially to the horse culture people, as a Medicine Hat."

Photograph of San Domingo by Hope Ryden taken at the Brislawn Cayuse Ranch in 1969. San Domingo had a red roan floral or rosette mottling. In 1969 only six true Medicine Hats were in the Spanish Mustang Registry at that time.

San Domingo

During the 1960's a young Medicine Hat Stallion was brought in from the wild by some Navajo Indians at Santa Domingo Pueblo. They notified Robert Brislawn, of Oshoto, Wyoming. The moment he laid eyes on him, Brislawn named him San Domingo.

San Domingo was about 14.5 hands tall shown here with one of the Brislawn brothers. San Domingo remained half-wild. This was about as close as anyone could come to him.

Brislawn, along with his brother Ferdinand Brislawn of Gusher, Utah, owned a four thousand acre ranch they had named "Cayuse Ranch Preserve," near Oshoto Wyoming. This preserve, started in 1920, was the beginning of a fifty year search in the wilds for mustangs that appeared to carry untainted Spanish blood.

A <u>Medicine Hat</u>, Atseeh łįį', is a horse believed to possess powerful medicine, was believed to be a magical horse. Only the boldest members of the tribe, a brave who had proven he was worthy during a conflict would be allowed to ride this highly revered horse.

The <u>white man</u>, Bilagánaa, called this special horse a War Bonnet. He named it this because of very its special rare markings. A medicine hat or war bonnet horse has a mostly white body with solid colored ears that were marked in such a way they appeared to be wearing a war bonnet. A Medicine Hat must also have a dark shield of color covering its chest to "protect" against arrows and bullets. This horse is a type of color phase of the pinto, a Spanish Mustang. Beneath its coat flowed blood that was particularly hot and wild.

- In the Comanche tribe, Bitsii' yishbizhii, if a warrior earned the right to ride a Medicine Hat into battle, he considered himself <u>invincible</u>, doo bik'ehodidlíní.
- <u>Cheyenne</u>, Biłį́į' łikizhii – they believed a Medicine Hat horse was magical.
- <u>Lakota</u>, Anaałání kept these horse in numbers.
- <u>Black Feet</u>, Bikee' łizhinii Medicine Hats were possessed by this tribe also in great numbers during the 1860's.

Will Tsosie said: "Indian ponies, regardless of color markings were always able to outmaneuver the United States Calvary's taller, larger horses. Indian ponies regardless of how they were marked were better, stronger, faster <u>war horses</u>, anaa łį́į'."

It is a fact that the U.S. Calvary chose its mounts not only for conformation of body but for their color. Most often the Calvary wanted bay colored horses so the conformation of the riders would appear more unified. Their horses had to be at least fifteen hands or taller. This preference by the military for a horse of a certain color really was no different from an Indians choice of Pintos, Medicine Hats and <u>Appaloosas</u>, łį́į' tł'aaká a'ii.

Photograph by Hope Ryden taken in 1969 at the Cayuse Ranch. San Domingo feels threatened by another stallion and runs to challenge him.

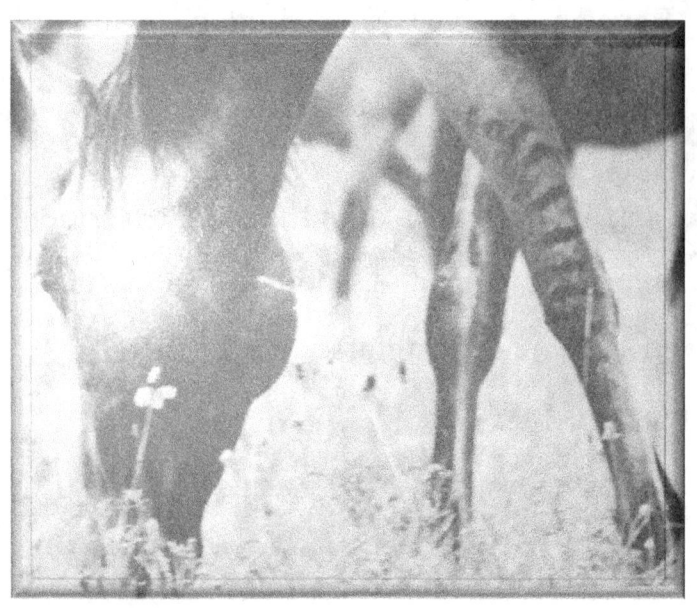

Photo by Hope Ryden

The Brislawn foundation stock was attained over a period of years by the two brothers from several bands of <u>wild horses</u>, łį́į́' ałchiní, from Oklahoma, New Mexico, Montana, Utah and Arizona. These horses were allowed to run free and live in a wild state on their Cayuse Ranch. Some of them had color gene patterns such as dorsal stripes crossed over the withers and zebra stripes on their legs.

These patters indicate a <u>reversion</u>, benáłt'éii, to more primitive horse coloration. These wild horses were developing camouflage. At this time, San Domingo was living on the Brislawn Cayuse Ranch with his band of seven mares. He sired five Medicine Hat fillies. A wild stallion will not permit one of his own fillies to remain in his herd after she had matured. Because of this San Domingo did not mate with any his female offspring.

It is easy to understand why different tribes believed these horses had mystic powers. San Domingo was totally aware of himself at all times. He was charged with personality. According to Robert Brislawn he was the most selective of the four stallions on the Cayuse Ranch in his choice of mares.

"No stallion was more possessive of his mares than was this Medicine Hat. It was never a good idea to approach San Domingo on horseback even when riding a gelding. San Domingo always met all comers ready for a fight, like the good war-horse that he was."

Some of the pure-blood descendants of the sixteenth-century animals ridden by Conquistadors have been <u>salvaged</u>, yisdááť'eezhígíí, from the wild and are in captivity. The Bureau of Land Management seems determined to remove all of these magnificent wild horses from the land they have lived on for over four centuries. Once they are gone from the wild, they will be gone forever.

Robert Brislawn was convinced that man's most recent efforts at tinkering with horses has resulted only in the breeding down of the animal, and that nature is a better horse breeder than modern man. Wild stallions will expel their fillies from their individual bands and <u>harems</u>, łį́į́sa'ii, of mares when these fillies reach a year of age. What mysterious <u>mechanism</u>, t'áá bíniik'eh ánáť'įįh, of nature triggers this reaction that keeps these stallions from mating with their daughters is unknown. When these stallions are left alone to organize their own social units, the practice of "line breeding" commonly employed by <u>professional horse breeders</u>, łį́į' bííyisii, does not occur naturally in nature among horses.

The blood of these rare horses stills flows in the veins of the wild horses that are in scattered bands throughout the West. A herd of wild Mexican-bred Spanish horses was found living on the Wilbur Cruce Ranch near Arivaca, Arizona in 1989. These horses were still running free together wild and pure, concealed from time by the remoteness of the Wilbur-Cruce Ranch. The herd numbered one hundred in the winter of 1989, but by the time the horses were taken off the land some months later, their numbers had dwindled to seventy-seven. I don't know what happened to them.

A biologist for the U.S. Fish and Wildlife believed that some of the twenty-three missing animals were taken by thieves, most likely to haul drugs up from Mexico. But many more were being killed by mountains lions. Because of the drought, the horses had gathered at the only remaining watering hole, Arivaca Creek that was making them easy targets for hungry cats. Should these horses have been left alone? Is this is the way it should be in the wild, nature's way of keeping everything balanced. Does that work well? If man gets involved is his way better than nature?

Experts from the Spanish Mustang registry and the American Minor Breeds Conservancy were summoned to examine the horses. Blood was drawn to determine if it contained the genetic traits of the Spanish breed. The results were positive.

This was a rare find. In many cases, these horses blood has been diluted by the blood of other strains during the three and half centuries that have elapsed. Since that time many domestic horses, łį́į́' bee ak'ehodeesdlį́'ígíí, heard the cry of the mustangs and joined them by escaping or being set free. Renegades from the United States Calvary, runaways from ranches, and old favorites simply turned out to pasture.

It is interesting that the Spanish horse's, Naakii biłį́į́', traits frequently emerge in animals of a little as one thirty-second Spanish ancestry. The Spanish genes are apparently so persistent that even a random mating between two wild horses of obviously mixed ancestry will sometimes produce a colt that confounds observers by appearing to be pure Spanish in all details.

The Argument: Were horses always here?

For generations before the Northern tribes ever saw a white man they possessed many horses on the Plains. A <u>Paiute</u>, Béyoodzin, elder in Yerington, Nevada recalled the stories of horses told to him by his grandfather:

"Far back as I heard they were here. I heard people say they came from the Spaniards. The white people say that. But the Indian says the horses were here. They are our horses. <u>Spotted,</u> neestł'in, and all color of horses. That's all I heard. I've heard as far back as I can remember from the old folks who use to talk about them. The real Indian pony is the little, short, chunky one . . . low to the ground, they told me, 'short and chunky, the real Indian pony. There's a lot of them that were never broke and running all over, they told me, here, there, and in Smith Valley, and all around."

The period from 1640 to 1880 has been called by anthropologists the period of the Indian horse culture. During this time wild horse bands multiplied without interference on the frontier despite the advancing settlers. It is little wonder that Indian tribes could not credit the white man with bringing them the horse.

When Marquette journeyed west of the Mississippi in 1673, the first Indians who greeted him were already riding horses. One wild-horse expert, Kent Gergersen, a founder of the National Mustang Association, believes the Paiute Indians are correct in their belief that the horse was "always here." He thinks the Indians may have coexisted with the wild horse without attempting to tame or ride it. Historians who feel that the Indians had never seen a horse merely because the tribes expressed terror at the sight of the mounted Conquistadors may not have understood that it was the men who were riding the horses which case the Indians' alarm.

Gergersen says: "You can't make me believe the Indians would think of riding a buffalo or a bull elk either at least until they'd seen someone else do it."

Gergersen also said: "From the late 1930s to the early 1950s there were from 3,000 to 4,000 wild horses in the Utah area, and most were caught by wranglers for the meat market. Many ranchers turned domestic stallions in with the wild Mustangs to try and increase the size of the horses and keep the attributes through cross breeding. The little mustang studs would kill the domestic' stallions, and those that survived didn't adapt. They got sore footed, got down in condition, and winter killed. So, there was retention of the original blood lines. Likewise," he said, "domestic horses didn't want to mix with the Spanish type horses."

Around 1816 a youthful adventurer, Ross Cox, trapper and fur trader, recorder the following observations in his Columbia River Journal:

"They (the Indians) are hard taskmasters and the hair rope bridles, with the padded deerskin saddles, which they use, lacerate the mouths and backs of the unfortunate animals in such a manner as to render them at times objects of commiseration . . . In summer they (the horse) have no shelter from the heat, in winter no retreat from the cold. And their only provider throughout the year is the wild loose grass of the prairies, which in the latter season is generally covered with snow and the former is brown and arid, from the intense heat of the sun." Yet, he said, "Despite the hardness of their lives, the Indian ponies seemed to display the same strange attachment for their riders that the Indians had for their mounts."

Washington Irving, in Astoria, marvels at the way the animals preformed for their masters:

"It is said that the horses of the prairies seemed to readily distinguish an Indian from a white man by the smell, and he gives preference to the former. Yet, the Indians in general are hard riders and, however, they may value their horses, they treated them with roughness and neglect. Occasionally the Cheyenne joined other Indian hunters in the pursuit of buffalo and elk, and in the ardor of the chase, spared neither themselves nor their steeds, scouring the prairies at full speed, plunging down precipices and frightening ravines that threatened the necks of both horse and horseman, The Indian pony, well trained to the chase, seemed as mad as the rider and pursued the game as eagerly as if it were his natural prey, on the flesh of which he was to banquet."

There can be no doubt that a strong bond did exist between the Indian rider and his horse which made it extremely difficult for the native to part with even his poorest animal.

According to paleontologists, the ancient ancestor of the horse the tiny, four toes creature called Eohippus (Hyracotherium) was present some fifty million years ago in an area that is now known as the Western United States. Skeletons of Eohippus have been unearthed hear Mount Blanco in the Texas Panhandle, and abundant fossil remains have been found in rich Eocene beds in the Bighorn Basin in Wyoming. Eohippus bones have been found in both England and North American, but all <u>modern horses</u>, dííjį́įdi łį'gíí, are said to be lineal descendants of the American Eohippus. The science community holds that during the period of the Cenozoic era, the British Isles and North America were attached; they both formed part of the supercontinent of Laurasia. This includes North America, Greenland, and Europe north of the Alps and as far east as the Himalayas,

During this long period, certain land connections remained which permitted animals to migrate back and forth freely, and it was during this time that Eohippus simultaneously inhabited both what is now England and Texas. Later when the connecting land bridges were severed and European Eohippus was isolated from its American relatives, it took an evolutionary turn and ended in extinction. The North American creature gradually modified into what we know today as the horse.

Since the fossil remains of the horse at every stage of development, from the tiny primitive, ałk' idą́ą́'łį'ę́ę, Eohippus, to the giant form we are familiar with today, have been found only in what is now western United States, the horse, it must be concluded, is a native of North America.

Yet, according to the science community, by the time Columbus arrived the horse had been extinct for eight thousand years on the North American continent. Scientists agree that before this happened many members of the horse family migrated across the land bridge connecting Alaska and Siberia and entered Asia where they eventually sired many present day variations.

Archeologists P.S. Martin advances a theory that is widely accepted by the science community at the present time. He suggests that Paleolithic man may have had a hand in wiping out the native horses, camels, and mastodons as well. He says: "this extinction was postglacial in time and affected in the main of larger animals. The principal factor isolated as cause is the appearance of man." Anthropologists suggest that the pressure of hunting tribes on the edible species, combines with natural factors such as disease wiped out the horse and the camel.

This genus Equus, includes modern horses, zebras, and asses, is the only surviving genus in a once diverse family of horses that included 27 genera. The precise date of origin for the genus Equus is unknown, but evidence documents the dispersal of Equus from North America to Eurasia approximately 2 to 3 million years ago and a possible origin at about 3.4 to 3.9 million years ago. Following this original emigration, several extinctions occurred in North America, with additional migrations to Asia (presumably across the Bering Land Bridge), and return migrations back to North America, over time. The last North American extinction occurred between 13,000 and 11,000 years ago.

Critics of the idea that the North American wild horse is a native animal, using only paleontological data, assert that the species, E. caballus, which was introduced in 1519 by the Spanish, is a different species from the one that disappeared 13,000 to 11,000 years in North America. This is the crux of the debate.

A relatively new 27-year-old field of molecular biology, using mitochondrial-DNA analysis, has recently found that the modern horse is genetically equivalent to the E. lambei horse, according to fossil records, that represented the most recent Equus species in North America prior to extinction. Not only is E. caballus genetically equivalent to E. lambei, but no evidence exists for the origin of E. caballus anywhere except in North America.

Horses, according to this data then are native species and must be protected.

BLM - Bureau of Land Management

To illustrate my point I have included some current issues plaguing the wild horses of today. A lawsuit cited not long ago by researchers who say the most recent science backs up the fact that horses are a native species to the Western United States and that this concept is now widely accepted by most of the scientific community.

The only ones who do not believe this is the BLM itself.

What do you think?

- American history textbooks teach generation after generation that wild horses are the result of European explorers and settlers who came across the ocean and into the frontier.
  - This theory is being challenged at archaeological digs:
  - In university labs
  - In federal courtrooms
  - Horse advocates battle U.S. government over BLM roundups
  - They say thousands of mustangs have legal and native claim to land.
  - A case was presented to the 9th U.S. Circuit Court of Appeals
  - The case maintained wild horses roamed the West 1.5 million years ago
  - It said that horses didn't disappear until 7,600 years ago
  - DNA evidence shows mustangs are genetically linked to ancient ancestors
  - Case says BLM treats wild mustangs as invasive and want them eradicated
  - BLM maintains horse advocates perpetuate a myth

- Many cattle and sheep ranchers claim its part of a ploy to push livestock off public lands.

- BLM says it's a "false claim" that wild horses are native to the United States. "American wild horses are descended from domestic horses, some of which were brought over by European explorers in the late 15th and 16th centuries, plus others that were imported from Europe and were released or escaped captivity in modern times," it says.

- BLM says: "The disappearance of the horse from the Western Hemisphere for 10,000 years supports the position that today's wild horses cannot be considered `native' in any meaningful historical sense."

- BLM acknowledges horses have adapted successfully to the Western range, but biologically they did not evolve on the North American continent.

- A director of Zoo Montana's Science and Conservation Center in Billings, Mont. says BLM's view is outdated.

- He says, "On the face of the science, it is just absolutely incorrect," zoo director studied reproductive physiology for decades since earning a degree at the College of Veterinary Medicine at Cornell University.

- "It wasn't the predominant horse on the continent but it was here. It is native to North America," he said. "This isn't about history, it's about biology. The Spanish were simply bringing them home."

- Curator of the Department of Mammalogy at the American Museum of Natural History in New York agrees. He said mustangs are classified as Equus caballus, which evolved from primitive forebears in North America.

- "No question that horses are `native' within any reasonable meaning of that word – much more so than bison, for example, whose immediate ancestry is Asian." He said.

- "Yes, it disappeared from our shores for a few thousand years, but that has no bearing scientifically on whether it is historically `native." He said.

- An executive director of the Wildlife Society, a non for profit scientific and educational association in Bethesda, Md. disagrees.

- "Horses did evolve in North America but they went extinct 10,000 years ago," he said.

- "Today's mustangs are a domesticated, feral version that went through many generations of selective breeding to use as beasts of burden and were brought back to North America. They are a mishmash of domestic horses. They are not native. They are not wild horses."

- If horse advocates win any lawsuit in court it would help determine the future in the management of mustangs. A court win has the potential to send BLM back to the scientific drawing board before any seasonal roundups resume of thousands of mustangs that they say are damaging the environment.

- BLM agrees Congress wants the horses treated as part of the environment but focus should be on protecting the land not affording horse's special treatment.

- "They are not an endangered species," BLM said. "The effect on the horses themselves would be part of the environmental study ... but the ultimate question is, `Does this proposal bring about a significant environmental impact?"

- The purpose of the wild horse and burro act is to protect wild horses from capture, harassment, branding and death.

- Lands were designated for horses with this law – mustangs are an icon of the West, an embodiment of freedom – should the BLM make a priority out of protecting them?

What do you think? Discuss these points in class?

Higher level thinking questions for discussion:

- Do you think the Bureau of Land Management or BLM agency misinterprets the law regarding the protection of wild horses?

- Do you think these wild mustangs are native species and should we protect them?

- Why aren't wild horses and burros better protected today under the Wild and Free Roaming Burro Act of 1971? What do you think has happened?

- The Wild Horse and Burro Act have been challenged numerous times in courts up to the level of the Supreme Court, and have been upheld in all instances. Charges have also been made that the BLM has turned a blind eye to the practice of private investors adopting feral horses for the purposes of slaughter, and courts have determined that the BLM may not ignore the intent of adopters. Do you think the BLM is not following this law? Do you think they are following the law?

- Whatever your opinion or view is on these issues, do you feel that you have a civic duty to express your opinion to the BLM?

- Or to your congressmen about this issue?

Wild horses: BLM facts and figures

- U.S. Bureau of Land Management manages 245 million acres of federal land.

- This land is in 12 western states.

- 30 million acres is now designated as horse management areas in 10 states

- Horse management under Wild Free-Roaming Horse Burro Act of 1971

- This act was signed into law by President Nixon.

- There are 10 states that have wild horses

- Arizona, California, Colorado, Idaho, Montana, Nevada, New Mexico, Oregon, Utah and Wyoming.

- About 33,000 horses currently roam the 10 states, (this was in 2011)

- Roughly half of those are in Nevada, with another 5,500 burros

- Total of about 38,500 animals under the U.S. Bureau of Land Management.

- BLM maintains it's about 12,000 more than the rangeland can sustain

- They plan to roundup most of these horses to get to their management level they set for the current year at 26,600.

- In 2010 the BLM removed 9,715 horses and 540 burros from the range.

- BLM has 41,700 wild horses and burros in short term corrals they removed

- 13,100 of these are in short-term corral holding pens in the West.

- In long-term pastures in Midwest they have about 28,600 horses and burros.

- BLM spent $67 million on wild horse burro program for the 2010 fiscal year

- $37 million of that is to keep animals in holding facilities taken from range.

WHAT IS A MUSTANG?

Wild horses in Arizona

In the year A.D. 711, the Moors invaded and conquered Spain on the backs of <u>vigorous,</u> bidziilii, horses born to survive the inhospitable deserts of North Africa. These Bedouin Arabian horses were small, but tough. We call them hot blood horses. They had fast reflexes and were well suited for combat.

These invaders, bent on <u>proselytizing</u>, biyahozhniiłįįh, (preaching their beliefs) for Islam and Allah, regarded their desert war horses as sacred, and they treated them accordingly. Moorish warriors had an attitude towards animals in general that was unsentimental, sometimes brutal. With these horses they did have these beliefs instead they felt that their war-horses were not animals at all, but more like trusted allies in holy battle.

Moors had no compassion for weak, old, injured, or otherwise <u>imperfect horses,</u> łįįchxǫ'í, but they were said to displayed more preference for a <u>fit horse</u>, łįį' bííyisii, than for their women or their families.

At this same time, Spaniards were riding heavy <u>European horses</u>, Tóhónaa łįį'. These horses were by contrast large, slow, and sturdy, having been bred to carry the weight of the armor-clad knights of the middle Ages.

The Moors wore their light weight attire that put no extra strain on their swift and <u>delicate</u>, bąąh hą́ą́h hasinígíí, horses. Consequently, the Moorish invaders easily outmaneuvered the thick-legged, heavily muscled animals from Europe, and the result was victory for the Moors. This hot-blooded horse of the Moors from North Africa affected the course of Spain's history. The horse could be traced to a mixture of Arabian and Barb stock.

A Barb horse is an offshoot of the <u>Arabian horse</u>, Séítah łį́į', developed by Libyans at an unknown earlier date. Barb horses over time lost their nice looks from the severity of living in North Africa. So, the Moors reintroduced more Arabian blood into their horses. The North African war-horse in time recovered much of its handsome appearance. Now their Arabian horse was viewed by many as the unparalleled beauty of the equine world. These horses possessed not only beauty, but intelligence, courage, and strength.

The Spaniards, recognizing the superiority of their <u>conquerors horses</u>, łį́į' bee ak'ehodeesdlį́'ígíí, set out to breed a <u>smaller horse</u>, łį́į' t'áá álts'ísígíí, for themselves. They added a touch of their own horse, especially the Norse dun horse then cross bred this Norse dun with the Arabian Bard mixture of the Moors and they produced the Jennet.

The jennet horse was a slightly larger animal, a horse with such distinctive qualities, intelligence, and speed that for the next eight hundred years Andalusia and Seville were renowned throughout the civilized world for their superior animals. This is the horse that the first Spanish explorers brought with them to the New World.

Today in the wild mustang horse bands, at least of those that are left still running free, it is possible for one to see Barb horse characteristics in one animal, while in the animal running next to it you may see qualities that are distinctively Arabian.

The facial profile of these horses reflects their Spanish ancestry with most showing a convex curving profile instead the straight profile usually what is normal in mixed breed horses. In the Spanish Mustang the mouth is shallow with a very refined muzzle and crescent shaped nostrils with curved ears that have a notch. Their throatlatch is well defined and they have a moderate length neck that blends into their well-defined withers. The neck on either a male or a female is well arched, which is another indication of their Spanish ancestry.

When one sees the chest of a Spanish Mustang it is strongly built and what would be considered a medium width but they have a definite "V" between their forelegs. The mustang's legs are strong, with short, sturdy, round cannons.

Chestnuts, remnants of toes on the legs, are small and smooth and may be absent on the rear legs. Ergots, a small callosity, or thickened callus, on the underside of the fetlock on these Mustangs are small or even absent. Spanish Mustangs are remarkably free of hoof and leg problems.

Their heart girth is deep the croup is rounded with hip bones well set in. Tail set is medium to low. Manes and tails are usually full and many of these horses have thick double manes. Their hind legs are set well under them which contribute to their well-known agility. Many Spanish Mustangs are inherently gaited. In addition to the normal gaits, they do a lateral pace step.

In the facial features on these horses, if one has a roman nose it is thought to be from a Barb horse influence; while the slightly dished face is an Arabian horse influence. This blend of Barb, Arabian and the Norse dun is referred to as an Andaluz mustang, łį́į' yázhí.

According to the Spanish Mustang Registry, the Andaluz is a <u>small horse</u>, łį́į' yázhí, by modern standards, with very intelligent quizzical eyes set widely apart, and separated by a flat forehead. The profile of its face is either straight or slightly dished and its small ears are pointed inward with a gracefully tapered muzzle and delicately shaped slanted nostrils.

The Andaluz mustang is high in the withers and long in the shoulder a very sturdy animal most often seen standing with round strong front legs held in a stiff posture which emphasizes its deep but narrow chest that shows a deep V under their chest. This is due to good solid musculature. The back is short like an Arabian's because it inherited the spine of its ancestor whose backbone lacked one vertebra.

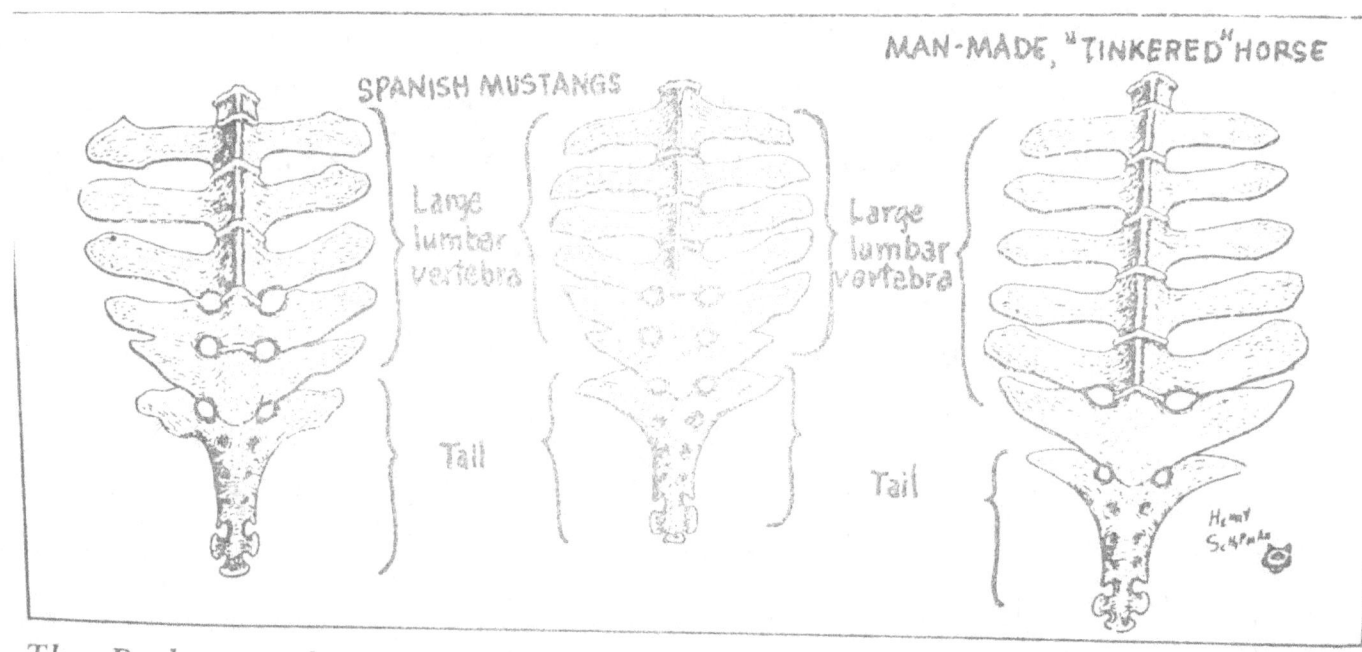

The Barb type has 5 large lumbar vertebrae.

The Andalusian type shows 5½ (or 5 and a piece) large lumbar vertebrae.

Modern breeds of to-day, except the Arabian, have 6 large lumbar vertebrae.

Drawing by: Henry Schipma

By contrast, a pure bred Spanish Jennet, first cousins to America's wild horses are now the long legged, showy creatures of Spain known today as Andalusians. They no longer resemble the prized sixteenth century horses of the Spanish conquistadors.

Today, most surviving wild horses live in desert states of the United States and are descendants of the stock that were kept by the Great Basin Tribes.

According to a BLM, Bureau of Land Management survey, nearly half the wild horses that originally roamed the land were estimated to be on open public lands that belong to the collective people of the United States. Does the BLM think they all need to be removed? What is there policy?

If enough people say they believe these horses should be allowed to live wild and free, as they have for over four hundred years, do you think that might make a difference? So far, the BLM continue rounding up and eliminating these strong mustangs. They take them to holding pens in the Midwest. Do you think these horses might be unaccustomed to living there? These lush Midwest plains, through preferred by the horses for the grasses, have been so exploited, yee ák'eesdla', and appropriated, ádii'yideeshchį, by the white man for his own use that many wild animals cannot survive there any longer. There just isn't any room for them.

The American wild horse is part of our heritage, part of our colorful past. Should they be forcibly removed from the land they've lived on for over four hundred years? Or should they be left alone? What do you think is the right thing to do?

As far as the question, was the horse here before the Spaniards came, the answer is yes they were according to the new DNA tests. They are linked to the prehistoric natives that evolved on this continent and regardless of how this little horse got back to America it has a romantic history that binds us as a nation together like glue.

It is agreed that the wild mustang that ran in huge herds across the western prairies of our great land in the past that it was given the name of "mestenos," which means a stray or ownerless horse, by the Spanish. This is why we call them Mustang today.

The Spanish Mustang Registry, established in 1958 by the Brislawn family, was set up as a non-profit venture. Its purpose was to solely perpetuate, béé hániihgo, the mustang and to establish a permanent reserve for a national treasure and heritage, bits'áádóó anoot'įįłii, for the people of the United States. Do you agree with that?

The story of the wild mustang in North America is the subject of "La Primera," a song written and performed by Canadian folk singer and horse enthusiast, by the name of Ian Tyson.

In his song he sings the words: ". . . and he became an outlaw and his blood was watered some, but the flame still burns into the new millennium."

Questions for Consideration

1. There is a difference of opinion between the science community and Native American communities on whether the horse was here before the Europeans arrived. What is your opinion on this?

2. Why does the Mustang have one less lumbar vertebra in its back?

3. Do other horses of today have this? If so what is that other breed?

4. What do you think we mean when we say that some of these horse are reverting back to a more primitive color pattern?

5. How or why might this happen?

6. What is a Medicine Hat? Describe this horse and what makes it so different.

7. Why was this particular horse so sought out by different Native American tribes?

8. What is the land bridge that was during the Ice Age? How long ago was that?

9. Do you think that a wild horse should be allowed to remain free? Or should they all be captured and sold or adopted? Why?

10. What is meant when someone says the mustang horse is part of our national heritage?

11. Are horses native to this continent?

12. What is your favorite color of horse and why?

13. Name the Plains Indians Tribes that were considered to be the horse-culture tribes.

14. Where does the word mustang come from? What does the word mean?

15. When the Moors conquered Spain what kind of horse were they riding?

16. What gave the Moors an advantage?

17. What horse or horses played an important role in what the mustang is today?

Navajo words found in this text

1. horse	łį́į'	pg. 10
2. obsidian	bááshzhinii	pg. 15
3. turquoise	dootł'izhii	pg. 15
4. abalone	diichiłí	pg. 14
5. white shell	yoołgaii	pg. 14
6. wealth	jit'į́	pg. 10
7. material goods	naalyéhé	pg. 15
8. knowledge	baa ákohonidzinii	pg. 15
9. East	Ha'a'aah	pg. 14
10. South	Shá'diááh	pg. 14
11. West	E'e'aah	pg. 14
12. North	Nahookǫs	pg. 14
13. white horse	łį́į́łgaii	pg. 14
14. buckskin	anání	pg. 14
15. yellow	łitso	pg. 14
16. gray horse	łį́į' łibéíí	pg. 14
17. Blue Bead	Dootł'izhii yoo'	pg. 14
18. Abalone Shell	Dook'o'osłííd	pg. 14
19. black horse	łį́į́zhiin	pg. 14
20. jet	bááhzhinii	pg. 14
21. obsidian	bááshzhinii	pg. 14
22. pinto horse	łį́į́łkiizh	pg. 15
23. Chinle	Ch'ínlį́	pg. 15
24. composite	yee hadít'éii	pg. 15
25. Plains Indians	Bikágí yishtł' izhii dine'í pg.11	

Bibliography

1. Ryden, Hope. "America's Last Wild Horses," Sept. 20 1969. E.P. Dutton & Company

(Permission granted to use photographs of San Domingo in 1995 in first edition)

2. Benton, Michael. "Four Feet on the Ground," 1993. W.W. Norton & Company, Inc.

3. Spanish Mustang News: issue 17 pages 9-10

4. Banks, Leo W., Arizona Highways Magazine. "The Horses of History," November 1995, pgs.18-22

5. Interview with Will Tsosie, Tsaile College.

www.ingramcontent.com/pod-product-compliance
Lightning Source LLC
Chambersburg PA
CBHW080341290526

45791CB00009BA/2689